Yucaipa and My White Privilege

*How escaping the bubble helped me
understand the whole picture*

Cheryl Ann Hunter

Dedication

This book is dedicated to my family and friends, all of whom are part of the good and beautiful life in Yucaipa, California. It is dedicated to those who may have experienced harassment and mistreatment, or who feel unwanted. It is also dedicated to those who continue to strive for a better community, one that is inclusive and safe. Thank you, to those who understand and work toward a peaceful, inclusive, and equal way of living.

Preface

The year 2020 will be remembered as a year of strangeness. Our complacency as United States citizens led to our being shocked and ill-prepared for the challenges we were faced with. I turned 60, and finally graduated from college. Me, like many others in the first half of the year, felt cheated out of our deserved celebrations as a spreading pandemic that crippled the world necessitated new social behavior.

Our lives were disrupted, as citizens were advised to stay home, businesses were asked to close, and school moved to virtual online learning. Fortunately, I was able to work from home and my husband was able to continue with his business. Not everyone was so lucky, many lost their jobs, were furloughed, or had to close their business. There was the anxiety over the virus itself, the unknown future for our normality and sudden changes that pushed us to our emotional limits.

For months we struggled as businesses, schools, medical facilities and everything in our daily lives adjusted to wearing masks, social distancing, quarantine and working from home in an effort to stop the spread of the new deadly strain of the coronavirus known as COVID-19.

As if that were not enough, on May 25th a man named George Floyd was killed by police officer Derek Chauvin during an arrest. Floyd, a 46-year-old man living in Minnesota was held face down by the officer using his knee to press on the man's neck. Within nine minutes George Floyd stopped moving and died. The three other officers involved offered no intervention or assistance to the dying young man in handcuffs. Mr. Floyd happened to be black, and the incident sparked an already loaded powder keg of frustration across the country which exploded into protests, clashes between citizens, destruction of property, and a final drawing back of the curtain that has attempted to cover racism for years.

This was not the first time our country experienced police brutality against a person of color. In fact, days before and days after the George Floyd incident there were multiple occurrences of unnecessary force and differential treatment of a person of color involved in an altercation with police. The ensuing protests and arguments divided the country once again between those who supported the police tactics and those who supported the Black Lives Matter movement.

By June 1 of 2020, many citizens were taking up arms to protect their businesses, homes, and public buildings from what they feared were crowds of protestors coming to take over and destroy their towns. While most protests and marches were peaceful, there were the regular provocateurs and exploiters who used vandalism, intimidation tactics and all out destruction to take advantage of the situation. The resulting spread of fear tore the country apart.

The escalation reached my hometown as the world watched a sleepy inland southern California city become the center of controversy surrounding racism, gun rights, freedom of speech and a long standing history of bigotry in a privileged bubble that is Yucaipa.

The purpose of this book is not to rehash the story of George Floyd or the weeks of protests and racial divide, nor is it to bash my hometown. It is to explain why Yucaipa was so easily marked as a symbol of white privilege. I know that many of my friends, relatives and acquaintances may find fault with my opinion, but it is just that, my opinion.

I remember at ten years old being naïve and curious about other cultures. I can pinpoint the first time I experienced the pain of empathy for a person of color. I remember the sadness I felt when my little brother (who is white) was bullied, teased, and called a "brown potato" by his classmates at Yucaipa Elementary school. I will expand on that later.

My primary purpose is to point out that the meaning behind white privilege is all about the bubble some of us live in, as it blinds us to the truth. We do not understand what others must go through simply to live their lives, never mind getting ahead. But I will also address the beauty and goodness of the special place that is Yucaipa. I love that little town, but sometimes it is like a relative that you love unconditionally yet cannot stand to be around. I know many will not finish reading this because they are still not able to understand and refuse to hold a mirror up and consider it.

Nothing will change until everything changes. That means we each have to look deep inside and be honest about what kind of world we want to live in, who we blame for it not being what we want, and what we have done to contribute to the good, the bad and the ugly. We did not get to this point by chance, destiny, or divine plan. We got here because of fear, ignorance, hopelessness, and selfishness. In the end we will be remembered by how we lived and how we loved. I do not want our grandchildren to look back wondering why we wasted so much time fighting each other instead of creating a beautiful world that works for everyone. I have faith that we all will do better.

Cheryl, on her pony Patches
Yucaipa, California, 1968
(photo credit: Maude C. Bell)

Days of Carefree Innocence

It was 1966 when my family moved from Highland, California to Yucaipa. My dad worked for Standard Oil as a delivery driver. He was offered a Chevron gas station franchise in Calimesa, the neighboring town of Yucaipa. Unincorporated at the time, the area was full of farms, ranches, fruit trees and walnut groves. My parents rented out the home they owned in Highland and, in turn, rented a home in Yucaipa for $50 per month (I know, crazy huh?). The house was a ranch style with three bedrooms, one bath, sitting back away from the street on just over an acre of land. There was a large garage, a horse corral, barns, duck pond and chicken coop. An old pale green concrete grove cistern sat beneath a huge fig tree.

The place was paradise to me and my siblings. With trees to climb, an acre to run around on and an ever-growing menagerie of animals, we loved it. Eventually our place became nearly self-sustaining, with chickens, ducks, geese, vegetables, and fruit of all kinds we only needed to buy meat on occasion and had milk delivered.

When I was seven years old my parents bought a little pony for us to ride. Her name was Patches and she became my world. Within a year I was grooming her, washing her, cleaning her hooves, putting on the saddle and bridle myself and riding her around the corral or through the wash as often as possible. Those days were magic, and I would spend all day outside. I ate fresh fruit and vegetables, played with my brothers, helped with outside chores, and learned so much about growing our own food.

In that same year, my little sister came along. Born in 1967, she was the fourth child. She, like my younger brother, resembled my dad with her dark skin, dark hair and brown eyes. My other brother was fair with light hair like me.

My grandma, grandpa and great grandpa moved their trailer onto our property for a while. I learned to bake bread, knit, and sew from my mom and grandma. Great grandpa taught me a lot about horses and gave me handmade leather goods that he crafted while sitting in a chair under the large tree that hung over the trailer.

Mom decided to complete her GED and then go on to nursing school and achieve her dream of being a registered nurse. With school, a farm and four children under the age of eight, life was a challenge, but mom rose to meet it. I did not know until my adult years just how much my parents struggled to get by. I was always excited to get my older cousin's hand-me-down clothing, and for our annual trip to Sears for school clothes. Having my grandparents around was such a blessing, as my parents were able to have help with us kids and the farm upkeep. Dad worked twelve hours a day, six days a week at the station, and mom was going to school and studying. Mom stretched out her "allowance" to make sure we had everything we needed.

My dad's gas station was one of a few in the Yucaipa area at that time. It was busy and popular; he was a great mechanic. I loved going with him on the occasional Saturday to hang out. I would clean the bathroom, sweep, and clean the office and other light chores. I felt so proud to see my dad in his crisp uniform and black shiny shoes.

Between 1966 and 1970, I watched a man walk on the moon, the funeral of a great president, and the civil rights marches play out on a small black and white television. I walked to Calimesa Elementary school from first through fifth grade and can still remember some of my teachers and friends. I have no recollection of other races in my classrooms, but I had not been taught that there was a difference so I may not have noticed if there were any other races. Most probably, there were no other races at that school.

What I can recall is the cruelty of students and teachers against the kids who did not stand for the flag salute. There were quite a few of my school mates who came from families who were Jehovah's Witness. In their belief, the act of saluting the flag is honoring our country over the eternal one true government of God. One of my friends explained it to me and gave me a pamphlet to read. I shared it with my mother who explained that there are many ways to worship God. We did not go to church at that time, but we did talk about God and religion whenever there were questions. Sadly, I watched on many occasions as some of my friends were laughed at or talked to sternly by a teacher who made them stand up during the flag salute. I felt so sad inside.

During this time, I would occasionally confide in my grandmother about things that bothered me. She was my secret advisor for many years, and I have never forgotten the most important words of wisdom she shared. Unconditional love seemed to be the theme running through all her decisions, and I tried to apply that later in life once I understood it. My grandmother was the type of person who believed that all life is equally sacred. Of course, my mother did too, but grandma was very insistent about it. She was friendly toward everyone and welcomed anyone into our family. Grandma cared for her younger sisters and father while raising her own four children. In fact, she, my grandfather, great grandfather, four children and three sisters lived in a two-bedroom house in Yucaipa in the 1940s. They barely got by but knew how to make their resources stretch. Grandma made flour sack dresses for the girls to wear, made rag dolls for them to play with, and made do with whatever food they could grow or do odd jobs to buy.

My dad's family came to California from Oklahoma in the 1940s. They lived in a small travel trailer and tents, working as mechanics, farm workers, stone masonry, and other things. My parents met when mom's family moved a trailer into the same trailer park as dad's. They grew up together, and began dating while in high school, marrying in 1956. My dad went to work with Standard Oil, my mom dropped out of high school and I was their first born in 1960. Mom worked at a local hamburger stand until my brother's birth in 1961.

Our family's early story is like so many other vanilla stories across the country. Part of the white American culture is the pride in making something out of nothing, as self-made resilient pioneers spreading from coast to coast. While that is an admirable quality, the untold story of how colonial American rules and traditions favor that culture needs to be widely told and understood. When I was first introduced to the concept of "white privilege," I, like so many others, assumed it meant we were wealthy or that our life was easy. It took a few years to fully understand what the phrase really means. Being aware of the problem, or the root of the cause, is the first step toward improving the effect.

Yucaipa - A Brief History

Yucaipa was originally home to the Serrano people, who made flour from the acorns that fell from the abundant oak trees in the area. These indigenous people are believed to have inhabited the area for at least 2,500 years. The Yucaipa valley was an ideal area for meeting other groups, trade and settling disputes. In the 1700s Spanish invaders removed the Serrano people from their land and forced them into missions. Then, in 1842, Mexican Governor Alvarado granted Yucaipa land to Antonio Maria Lugo.

When California became a state in 1850, settlers from Utah bought the land from the Lugo family. They sold most of it off in parcels, thus forever changing the culture of the area. At the time, fruit trees and walnut trees were productive farming endeavors as Yucaipa became a supplier to much of southern California.

According to the Yucaipa Valley Historical Society, after WWII fruit farming gave way to trailer parks and chicken ranches. The website states, "Yucaipa underwent some major changes after the war. Fruit production diminished, and many of the former orchards were just the right size for trailer parks, chicken ranches and small housing tracts. In 1947 the first trailer park went in. By 1960 there were 50 such parks, though by that time they were known as mobile home estates, and Yucaipa became a retirement destination for many. The first housing tract was developed in 1947. Chicken ranches and egg production soon became our major industry."
(http://www.yucaipahistory.org/frm_yucaipa_history.htm).

The town was not incorporated as a city until 1989, I was a twenty-nine-year-old mother of two by then. The rural charm that attracted the ensuing masses of home buyers to the newly built Rolling Hills and Chapman Heights communities soon became their greatest complaint. The flies, the egg ranches, the horses, and other livestock that had been part of Yucaipa for generations, were now a problem to be addressed by the new property owners moving in droves to the quaint little valley town.

I remember as a teen riding horses with my friends to the store, the park, and up to Oak Glen. We were used to the flies, as would be anyone who grew up with livestock. By the 1990s, however, the loud voices of the new track homeowners pushed for regulations that resulted in many of our long-standing ranches to go out of business.

The little town was waking up from its sleepy country feel and stepping into a new era of suburban sprawl and commuters. There is nothing wrong with that, by the way, and Yucaipa is a beautiful place to live. For the most part, the communities that have replaced the groves and grassy fields are landscaped and filled with walking and riding trails. Change happens, and farming gives way to suburbia or industrial buildings. I was hoping that the new people would bring new attitudes and a more open-minded way of thought. That did not happen, however, and the city seemed to become more small-minded.

I was supportive of growth, because I felt that bringing in more businesses would help with the revenue necessary to improve the city streets, and the housing would bring more money into the schools via taxes. When I mentioned this to a friend, her answer was "That kind of growth will also bring undesirable people here. We'll have gangs and drug problems."

---Sigh---

What's interesting about that comment is the fact that the drug problem already existed. Marijuana and crystal meth or speed were widely used when I was in school in the 1970's and during my sister's years at Yucaipa High School in the 1980's. I have been told that heroin is now a major problem in my hometown.

There are so many beautiful aspects of the area. Rolling green hills, beautiful weather, amazing views of snowcapped mountains, a thirty-minute drive to snow resorts, lakes and camping...and much, much more. Yucaipa is a lovely place to live, and most of the people are hardworking, good family folk that respect their fellow humans. But there is a bubble of ignorance and apathy that needs to be removed. White privilege is all about locking one's white self away behind the gates of "I don't see it so it doesn't exist." We can enjoy our lives and be proud of the lovely town we live in, and still be an advocate for change in the hateful attitude of racial bias.

Running From My White-ness

Growing up I was fascinated by the Native American culture. I wanted to be part of that culture, and spent hours researching my dad's family trying to find a connection that would prove my Native American bloodline. Though looking at my father, sister and brother one could plainly see some interesting colorful influence on our family gene pool, we have no trace of Native American DNA, a small amount connecting me to Portugal, Spain and Morocco, with a slight trace from the Caucasus. The other 98% is from Western Europe, made up primarily of English and Scottish. Why does this matter to me? Should this matter to me?

Somehow early in childhood I recognized and became fascinated by the differences in the faces I was seeing on television or in places outside my small-town bubble. That helped to open my mind to different cultures, but I now realize that the empathy I developed was misdirected by a watered down and outright censored education. My mother and grandmother were influential in shaping us with an open heart when it comes to all life, they were advocates for racial harmony and wholly against discrimination. I am grateful for the teachings of my mother and grandmother but regret the lack of exposure to other cultures during my childhood. This lack of exposure led to an amusing ignorant understanding of other people. Let me share an example.

As a teenager I was in love with the Jackson 5. I had all their records and wanted to marry Michael. My little sister was influenced by that as well. One day our family went to an out of town football game to watch my brothers play while my sister and I cheered with our cheerleading squad on the sidelines. Our team was primarily white with a sprinkling of Hispanic, the other football team was entirely black. There was a large family sitting near us with the opposing team. When my six-year-old sister saw them, she got very excited and yelled out, "Look mom, it's the Jackson 5!" My mom was horrified, she shushed my sister and smiled a shy apology to the family. My sister's reaction and our general response to anyone of color was born out of our fascination with them. All children are curious about difference, and unless that curiosity is tainted by a racist environment they will explore and learn about each other without preconception.

At that same football game, I took my little sister to the restroom which was packed with girls from the other team's cheerleading squad. We walked in the door, they stopped talking and stared at us. I smiled and said hello, then squeezed through them to take little sis to the stall. The silence was uncomfortable, but soon my sister finished and walked out to wash her hands. As we stood there, two of the girls came to the sink and asked if they could touch our hair. My hair was long, brown, and straight, my sister had soft natural curls almost black in color. The girls began to smooth our hair, talking about how long it was, play with different braiding techniques and discussing its texture. Then the other girls started to talk about their own hair and soon we were all talking about our hair, outfits, and cheerleading. We went back to the game and waved to each other across the field.

When you grow up in a sheltered bubble, without any negative influence regarding difference, you maintain that untainted acceptance of everyone. It is only when society or your family circle point out those differences that children form an opinion. Racism is learned. In addition, as in my case, without exposure to different cultures and the opportunity to interact with them regularly, it is difficult to develop a natural understanding of each other.

My three daughters are quite different in every way, but they also have had a common thread during their childhood. Each of them without prompting by anyone had a best or close friend in school who was black. Now this may not seem like an odd occurrence in California, but Yucaipa had a black population of 0.9% at the time. Thinking this over I realize that my sister and I may have influenced and encouraged our children with comments about equality, etc. over the years. This should be a good thing, right? But why does there need to be a reason for my children's open acceptance of any friend that resonates with them? Isn't this what I was trying to teach them? Did I influence them or were these natural friendships? Am I over-analyzing it?

Our family is quite diverse. I now have African American, Mexican, Filipino, Navajo, Romanian, Dutch, German, Hawaiian, Puerto Rican, and other mixtures in my extended family tree. This has helped me to realize that being in awe of such diversity may be racism on my part because I am emphasizing the difference. Just telling people about our family's diversity is like saying "I am not racist; I have a black friend." Yet, my reaction is born out of the experience of that small-town closed-minded mentality.

My niece and nephew are half Puerto Rican, and they had their share of social difficulties growing up in Yucaipa because of their dark skin and hair. I was angered time and again by the hateful comments thrown their way. Their mother, my little sister Wendy, endured comments about her choice of friends and mates. After dating a black man for a year or so she was referred to in our town as "that chick who dates black guys."

While attending elementary school in Yucaipa, my brother came home from his first day of kindergarten crying because the other kids called him "brown potato" due to his dark skin and hair. My sister and I have discussed this at length, and our adult children laugh at the emphasis we put on diversity. But what Wendy and I have concluded is that our under-exposure to diversity while growing up in a small white town, coupled with the philosophy taught by our family matriarch, made us *crusaders* instead of *educators* on the subject.

This crusader persona manifested in a big way when one of my daughters did not want to participate in a class project on family heritage because she was ashamed of that heritage. Most of her friends were Hispanic or mixed race and she felt embarrassed because of the history she represented. Because she has very light skin and light hair, I think they already knew her racial background, but she still tried to be something else. I remember her even saying to me, "I am ashamed to be white." This disturbed me because I wanted her to be proud of her ancestors, but I understood where she was coming from.

I do not share these things to honor any pain or plight, but to explain how my process to understand what white privilege is involves these notions. It is a journey to move from curiosity to pity, from pity to anger, from anger to guilt, from guilt to crusader, and finally from crusader to an understanding of white privilege and the obligation to share that with others. Guilt and crusading do not help anyone. Acknowledgment of white privilege and helping others to come to that understanding helps a lot.

Colonialism and Forced Assimilation

Many will argue that colonization and assimilation have been the method of progress, nation building and advancing civilization for centuries. While this is true, it does not make it right. Some aspects of colonization have been helpful in controlling disease, oppression, and cruel practices, but it has also destroyed entire cultures through genocide and enculturation. This has resulted in the loss of beneficial natural healing methods, building methods, languages and belief systems that served humanity well. The worst thing about colonialism is the subjugation of people. The very act of subjugation forever brands that population as "lesser-than." Even following emancipation or independence, the group will be affected by the lesser-than label for generations.

The stigma of being considered lesser-than is imprinted into the subconscious of people on both sides of the race issue. The offspring of those who conquer feel a sense of entitlement and are raised to believe that the "others" are less entitled, or somehow undeserving. The offspring of the people who have been conquered maintain an embedded belief that they cannot rise to the level of their fellow humans. Certainly, their belief is true in the sense that they have not always been allowed or supported in any effort to improve their existence. The hopeless cycle of white guilt and crusading efforts to make it easier for the oppressed, has only added to the problem. While some crusading led to new laws, more of the effort was poured into social programs. Instead of joining arm in arm through continued efforts to combat racism, never letting up, we became complacent after another social service bill was passed. This is what I now understand. While I am in complete support of social service systems, it is not the only answer to solving the inequality of our nation.

Colonialism sets up a society that operates to benefit the conquering people's agenda, beliefs, social system, economic system, and hierarchy. In the case of democratic, capitalistic systems, the eventual path to oligarchy begins to form. Once money is introduced into the governing body and partnerships form between the money makers and the lawmakers, the people are no longer in control. Government by the people, for the people should mean exactly what it states. Government systems should not be set up to benefit only the money makers.

The same may be said for cultural and religious systems. While some may choose to acclimate to a new way, no one should be forced to. Assimilation has had its positive effects throughout history, but most often it has caused the extinction of cultures rich with traditions that are bound up in their entire way of life. This disenfranchisement leads to a fractured sense of self. It takes many generations to overcome such loss. As the affected people try to regain their footing, they are chastised for lagging behind or not being able to measure up to the expectations of those who hold the cards.

What the European conquests and colonization did to indigenous inhabitants in the name of religion all over the world is an atrocity. The harm cannot be undone, but it can be a symbol of past behavior that we want to grow out of. The cruelty and inhumane treatment of our fellow beings as we stole what was theirs based on ignorant and greedy agendas, thinly veiled as manifest destiny, cannot be erased. But we can move to a higher purpose that may heal those wounds.

I want to assume that all can agree on the evils of slavery. But I am not so sure my peers have really considered the short span of time between the abolishment of slavery, civil rights and today. Civil rights came about in my early childhood. The Emancipation Proclamation was made into law in 1863, just twenty years before my great grandfather was born. This is fresh, it is a deep scar that permeates all sides. The encultured attitudes and social behaviors take more than a couple of generations to be modified. Some people harbor such deep beliefs or stigma that any shake up or change in their paradigm causes serious cognitive dissonance. Yet, only this type of wake-up call can lead to real change.

My schools were always well funded, and loaded with options for activities including music, sports, and educational excursions. It was not until later in life that I learned about the inequality in school experiences due to the funding system. I was also naive to the impact social and cultural community traditions had on the schools. For example: we cannot move forward as a country if children in one state are learning different versions of history from another. Students are receiving watered down lessons, with some leaving out important details entirely, certainly not helpful in educating our youth about their world. We need a more cohesive system at the federal level. We are beyond the days when states operated independently due to their different needs and cultural traditions. When it comes to education, especially in a digital world with immediate access to information, we should be united in what we believe to be true, and critical thinking should be taught from kindergarten.

Racism and classicism are not productive for any country. Eventually the system built on those two things will break down. Any government system that needs to dominate a segment of its people or allow money to be the determining factor in all decision making, cannot call itself a democracy.

An example of efforts to indoctrinate, and the struggle between two differing philosophies is found in the battle between the Yucaipa School Board and the parents. When my oldest daughter was in middle school, she loved the books *A Light in the Attic* and *Where the Sidewalk Ends* by Shel Silverstein. Yucaipa Unified School District introduced the new reading series *Impressions*, which contained some of Silverstein's poetry. Parents and religious leaders confronted the school board and demanded they choose a different series. Their complaints were based on their opinion that many of the stories and poems contained death, supernatural and vulgar themes. Perhaps it was because I loved the poems and stories myself, but I was one of the parents who thought the progressive approach of whole language with the *Impressions* series was good for my child. The fight between the conservative parent groups and the school board became big news.

The Los Angeles Times reported in an article on August 20, 1990 about the nationwide controversy written by Jennifer Warren, that "...But nowhere, national groups tracking the issue say, has the protest's ferocity matched the war engulfing Yucaipa, a small community of orange groves and ranch-style homes east of San Bernardino." National attention was focused on the small quiet bubble of Yucaipa.

The fight over this brilliant reading series continued and grew more volatile. Warren lists the following instances following the decision to vote for a recall of the school board members who voted in favor of the *Impressions* book:

> "Angry parents picketed various schools in the weeks after the board's decision, and some families have pulled their children out of the district in protest.

> Teachers, administrators, and school board members have received hate mail and threatening telephone calls. The district's curriculum coordinator, Paul Jessup, has even been grabbed by his tie and swung around by an irate parent.

> In some classrooms, students under orders from parents refused to open their Impressions books. On the playground, taunts flew back and forth, with some pro-Impressions parents reporting that their children had been called "anti-Christian" and book opponents saying their children had been treated as outcasts.

A handful of parents upset about the books caused disturbances in classrooms. Two threatened and harassed school personnel to the point where the district obtained temporary restraining orders against them from San Bernardino County Superior Court."

It seems I may have veered off topic here, but my intention is to provide an example of the power some have over the government to push a religious or moral agenda based on their beliefs, with no concern for anyone else's. The ignorance of their reasoning is glaring. First, with no clear comprehension of the deeper meaning and significance in some of the literary gems contained in that collection, they are pushing their own fears and judgement upon others. Public school is for the public, not one portion of the public. If other macabre and supernatural books are okay, why are these any different? It is obvious why, as clinical psychologist Dr. Paul Hauck from Davis, California put it: "These parents don't have the view that you teach children to think independently, they want a teacher who will sit down with the children and tell them what to think." (A War of Words, August 1990, EducationWeek.org).

Yucaipa is a microcosm of our entire nation when it comes to an agenda of control and indoctrination. Independent thinking is a dangerous thing to any group that is trying to maintain control over another. This is where colonialism, subjugation and forced assimilation lead to classism. And in our country, it seems the lighter the skin then the higher the class, at least in the deep consciousness of the established whole. There is a reason for holding back truth from people or shading it. The truth makes it difficult to manipulate certain situations or environments. It most certainly stands in the way of manipulating people.

Stereotype and Appropriation

My younger sister graduated from Yucaipa High School in 1986. My husband (at the time) and I were attending her ceremony and ran into a mutual friend that was an alumnus and now coach there. When he asked my husband who we were there to support, and learned it was my sister Wendy, the guy's response was, "Oh yeah, the chick who dates black guys."

Wendy was a basketball star at Yucaipa High School. She earned a college scholarship and went on to play in her freshman year at a community college. At that time, she spent a lot of time outside, swimming, going to the beach, etc., and her skin was very dark. She had a short haircut that accented her frizzy curls and had highlights on the dark brown color. When she started college her basketball teammates asked what she was mixed with. They did not believe she was Caucasian. She is 100% European according to her DNA, but her features do not support that.

Wendy told me about her experience with dating. Since she hung out with her teammates of color, no white guys approached her to date. In fact, one of the team coaches told her that if she hung out with or dated people of color, she would not be asked out by white guys. The male and female basketball teams spent a lot of time together, and Wendy dated a few of the black players. One guy accompanied her to our family Christmas Eve party. My grandmother went out of her way to make him feel welcome, as did everyone.

I remember feeling good about it, but also like it was something cool. Looking back, I realize that instead of it just being about my sister dating a college guy, it was all about her dating a *black* guy. At the time I thought we were so awake and progressive, without realizing that those feelings were privileged and racist no matter how heartfelt.

My young adult years were filled with dancing and funk/soul/R&B music. I loved to dance and was a big fan of such groups as Kool and the Gang, Earth Wind & Fire, Michael Jackson, Janet Jackson, and others. I was also a fan of rock music such as Jethro Tull, Pink Floyd, and Kansas. When it came to dancing, I learned every move I could from watching television dance shows. I especially like the way people on Soul Train danced. When Wendy introduced me to RAP in the early 1980s, I liked the poetry and rhythm. It was a fun time. Wendy and I would go dancing with friends and practice the moves we learned. The first time I had an experience with cultural appropriation, before I even knew it was a thing, was when we were at a dance club. My sister and I heard the song "Push-It" by Salt-N-Pepa start up and we jumped out on the dance floor. Soon there were two black women dancing next to us. They began to do what we call the "Molly Ringwald" (named after actress Molly Rinwald's dance moves from 1980's movies), white dancing in other words. I immediately got the point and felt extremely uncomfortable. They were laughing and looking at us, obviously sending a message. My brain could not really understand why, but I knew I felt embarrassed suddenly.

It was like a veil of naiveté was suddenly pulled off my face. It was the beginning of my journey to change. I had always considered myself to be the ultimate non-racist, but that moment was the first of many to push me into a new level of understanding. I'm sure that I probably thought, "Gee whiz, I was only dancing like that because I admire that dancing. Shouldn't they be honored and happy that I want to dance like them?" Uggghhh. Suddenly I was reminded about all the times I wanted to be Native American and braided my hair, wore beads and headbands, and did anything I could to make believe I was one of them. This was similar, in that I was so enamored with their culture that I tried to emulate them. But now I think that it is just one more thing to be taken from them.

Avoiding cultural appropriation is like walking on a balance beam. It is easy to fall into insult. I have always loved music that I can dance to, even as a child. I have always admired the music, natural life, and spirituality of historical Native Americans. I do not believe there is anything wrong with enjoying or admiring someone's cultural traditions or attributes, but there is a time and place for it, and a sense of respect is the key. This brings me to my youngest daughter.

She became interested in dancing and singing at age nine. Her music of choice was always Hip Hop, some Pop, R&B and RAP. She was a huge Destiny's Child fan and was able to go to attend a concert. From that moment on her dream was to be on stage and become the next Beyoncé. We supported her through the process. She began to write her own songs to beats that we would lease or buy online for her. In the early 2000s we found a producer to record her first original EP. It was all R&B with a couple of Pop tracks. During this time, she embraced the culture down to the clothing. She loved the sport look and knew everything about the authentic west coast vibe. At the time I was not thinking about cultural appropriation, I felt like she was just following her passion.

Her singing had progressed to a very impressive level, and her sound was on a par with other professionals. Then she began to explore poetry and RAP, developing a style while listening to various rappers. I remember playing one of her recordings to a work friend and was asked, "Is she black?" I hesitated to answer because I was not sure if they meant it literally or if it was sarcasm. This is when I realized that I was on a constant balance beam of right or wrong, fair, or unfair, etc. My daughter was truly passionate about her genre. She was talented regardless of race or culture, and we would support her no matter what. But the world might not be as understanding in her choice of genre, given her white Dutch and Scot-Irish heritage. In fact, it was her Yucaipa High School classmates who made life difficult from the get-go.

An introvert at age thirteen, she was not comfortable in middle school. She befriended a group of Hispanic kids who made her feel accepted. Only attracted to guys with dark skin, hair, and eyes, she was not interested in her white male classmates. I was not made aware until later, when she was in high school, how she was teased and berated for hanging out with "greasy Mexicans." Here we go again Yucaipa.

When she made the varsity cheer team, as a freshman, she spent a lot more time with the other cheerleaders due to strict and rigorous practice schedules. During those busy years she still worked on developing her music. Her cheer mates did not understand it, since they were not interested in the genre, and their lack of mutual interests made it a challenge to fit in socially. She could not wait to be done with school. Moving on with her music career was all she had her sight set on.

Stereotyping is another area of racism that most white people do not realize they practice. The obvious, blatant type is when we assume things about someone because of their race and what our enculturation has made us believe. Even with the best intentions we fall victim to it. I remember when I would pick up my daughter from elementary school and we would drive by a large mansion of a home looking out-of-place for the neighborhood. I was always curious about it, watching it being built and waiting to see who would live there. One day while driving past I saw a group of black children walking up the driveway of the house with their backpacks on. I was curious about it because I had been waiting to see who would own such a grand house.

When I mentioned it to a friend the next day, she said, "Oh, it's probably a boys' home or something."

Of course, I was immediately struck by her comment. I said, "Why, because there are black kids going inside a mansion?"

Her answer was equally stunning, "Either that or the parents sell drugs. How would they have a house like that otherwise?"

I found out later that the man who built the house was a black contractor and it was his family that lived there.

I cannot fault that friend too much. I caught myself a few years back smiling inside and feeling joyful when I saw a black family in a nice car or nice house, as if to suggest it is so uncommon. How condescending. Uggghhh, again.

Parenting

As parents, we generally want the same things for our children, happiness, success, safety, long lives. We are responsible for teaching them appropriate behavior, manners, how to recognize danger and stay safe. We all have different ways of going about parenting, based on our own upbringing, our philosophy and culture. The similarities stop there. But it took me awhile to understand that. It was not until I put myself between a male teen and his parents that I learned a hard lesson.

Remember the kids who lived in the mansion? One of them ended up a good friend of my oldest daughter and attended gymnastics classes at the gym my sister and I owned. He was talented and extremely attractive, with highly developed muscles and very dark skin. The kid spent so much time with us that he became like family. He confided in us that he was gay but could not come out because he feared what his parents would do. I had not met his parents, and only knew of them from their son's description.

As time went on, and the young man grew in his knowledge, he became a coach for us. One day he had not yet come in to teach his class and we began to worry. He finally showed up fifteen minutes late with a bloody lip and a swollen eye. When he saw me, he began to sob, so I took him into another room and talked with him a bit. It was an odd situation because he was seventeen years old, towering over me and sobbing like a little boy. He said that his dad had beat him because he told him he did not want to play rugby anymore, he wanted to take dance classes and become a professional dancer.

My first thought was to call Child Protective Services, but the young man begged us not to, saying he was planning to move out since he would be turning eighteen soon. He stayed with friends for a few days, then asked to stay with us. We offered him our couch for as long as he needed. After the first day I received a phone call from his father, with the mom on the line as well. They began to lecture me on minding my own business, and I began to defend myself in protecting their son. The conversation turned ugly when I started talking about my parenting philosophy without physical punishment. Mom lost it with me at that point and told me what it was like to raise a black child and how it was necessary to use tough love and make sure they understood the dangers for them in the world. Dad chimed in with stories about prison and asked me if I knew what "tossing a salad" means. I kind of guessed, but his detailed description made it clear. It was in this uncomfortable discussion of childrearing that I realized how different philosophies stem from such opposite circumstances, and that my sugary sweet world with time outs and reward systems may not apply in all families.

Looking back I can understand that the dad was trying to explain to me that when their son argues or talks back he needs to be put in his place, which is their effort at teaching him not to argue with authority. This was why he mentioned the prison part, because even though their son was a sweet kid, it would only take one argument with law enforcement to change his life forever...or maybe even lose it. Scaring him was their way of protecting him. And now I can see that the fear is real.

All these years later, that kid is now a grown man and he is successful. There was some tragedy along the way, including his father being murdered, but the kid managed to make it on his own. We are still in touch from time to time.

Living in a bubble, only seeing tragic things happen on television, the news or to other people outside your circle doesn't mean you can't feel sympathy, but it is difficult to have empathy when it is so far removed that it doesn't seem real. It hits home when you are affected by it.

When my sister and I had our gymnastics business at a storefront location, it was on a main street with constant traffic and passersby. My sister's daughter, my niece, was working as one of our coaches. After classes one evening, she and my daughter were hanging outside in front of the gym while we closed. It was a summer evening and we had the doors open. I heard some yelling and saw a pickup truck stopped in front with a group of young white men with shaved heads. They were yelling expletives at my niece and throwing things. My husband jumped in his truck and chased them. He told me later that he followed them to a house and got out to warn them not to come near us again. A few nights later, there were racial slurs written in white paint all over our windows. This was Yucaipa in 2004.

As a parent, my sister has exposed her kids to a broad range of cultural and social experiences. Her daughter is dark, with curly black hair, assumed by most to be black. Her son is tall and lighter skinned with straight thick black hair, assumed by most to be Hispanic. As previously noted, they are both half Puerto Rican. The kids' dad grew up in the Bronx, New York raised by parents who were involved with drugs and ended up in prison. Consequently, as a teen he was sent to live with his aunt in Riverside. He and my sister met in college.

His heavy Bronx accent and joking demeanor has always been charming, but his constant use of the "N" word is off-putting. I grew up learning that that is a word no one should ever say. In fact, in our family it was worse than the "F" word. I still cringe when I hear it. There it is again, my projecting white perception into a person of color's world. Of course, it is a negative word, of course I would never use it, yes, it is offensive to many. Yet it is a word that belongs to a culture, derived from a negative epithet forever linked to them. Their choice to use it is meant only for them to understand and none of my business. The kids grew up in two completely different households. Their dad leaned toward harsh physical punishment and expectations, while mom was a little more hands off and open minded. My sister's challenge was to help the kids feel comfortable in both worlds.

Unconditional love is the key to good parenting. This can be established in a house that uses physical punishment as well as in a house that does not. I may not agree with the type of parenting another uses, but I can respect it if I see that love is being shown along with it. This is probably the one thing I have had the most difficult time reconciling, but I continue to work on it.

My niece enjoys Rock, Folk and Indie music, while my daughter is into Hip Hop / RAP / R&B. They look like they should be the opposite based on stereotyping. The two of them are close, having grown up together spending hours at our house or the gym. My sister has had to console my niece on many occasions when she was left out of something, or when people tried to hook her up with the only black guy in school, or when she and the only other black cheerleader were set as bookends in the team photo. Parenting a child of color is delicate, being white and ignorant about the culture makes it especially challenging.

It is a great responsibility we have in helping our children learn to be proud of their country, while fighting for justice and equality. As noted in the chapter 2, "Running From My White-ness," the disjointed lessons of patriotic pride and historical inequality become difficult to reconcile. I remember trying to wrap my head around an unfair and disturbing incident involving my niece, two of our male coaches and a professional circus they wanted to audition for.

My sister and I had contracted with an acrobatic circus owner to allow them to use our gym and teach classes for us. The owner mentioned that she would audition youth that showed talent. Three of our coaches were extremely talented, and in fact my niece was taking a few of the circus classes. The two males were accomplished gymnasts and extraordinarily strong. One was

African American, the other was Hmong. When I mentioned them to the circus owner, she said that they were "too exotic" for the theme of the show, which had a patriotic name. I was dumbfounded. Did she mean that? Was "too exotic" another way of saying "too ethnic?" My relationship with this person began to spiral following that, and due to our need to downsize and some business disagreements, we parted ways.

How could I share the truth with my niece and my two coaches? I felt like a parent having to tell my kids that their favorite relative is a horrible person.

Leaving the Bubble

In January 2015, my husband and I bought a house in the desert and left our hometown of Yucaipa. My mom and sister still live there, and we go back weekly to visit. It is only a forty-minute drive, but it seems worlds away.

This first thing I noticed once we were settled, was the diversity. My maiden trip to the grocery store was such a different experience. Of course, my youngest daughter teases me about that. She lived in Los Angeles for a few years. I have explained to her that it was like waking up from a dream and being back in reality. I felt like I was part of the real world.

I realize that my reaction sounds so naive and privileged, and I apologize if it makes readers roll their eyes, but it is my truth. Maybe it is part of that white guilt still hanging on, I do not know. The one thing I can say is that regardless of why I felt so free, the experience of being in the open air of the desert, with diversity in every way all around me was exhilarating. Consider the fact that we now lived near one of the most densely populated areas of LGBT citizens (Palm Springs), and in a city where the white population is not the majority. Yucaipa was largely unaccepting of the LGBT community, and a majority white population. And though things there have begun to shift, the roots and attitudes of those influential folks still in control are deeply conservative regarding social issues. While I'm not suggesting everyone in Yucaipa is racist, I do believe that the majority of my hometown citizens do not understand white privilege or that without guidance, the bubble they live in does their children a disservice.

Interestingly, my husband and I brought our smiling, sugary polite white attitudes into an environment of people who are not necessarily used to our social niceties. When we would allow someone to go in front of us at the grocery store, or hold a door for them, the look of shock was noticeable. It has changed since then, maybe because we are just blending in now, or maybe we are not looking for those things anymore. We just feel part of the community now. With every size, shape, color, culture, economic class, etc. shopping alongside us, we feel more like Americans.

Our visits to Yucaipa are beginning to reveal a changing population lately. There are more people of color than ever before, and according to the city's demographics as reported by the World Population Review, on their website for 2020 Yucaipa population (https://worldpopulationreview.com/us-cities/yucaipa-ca-population/), 41% of black high school graduates have achieved Bachelor's degrees compared to 25% of white high school graduates in Yucaipa. This does not make a difference with regard to how they are treated or looked upon, however. I must admit, it still does my heart good to see more families of color contributing to the beauty of Yucaipa. Rich culture and diverse talents only enhance an already lovely place.

Leaving the bubble has allowed me to just be me. I grew up in an environment of achieving anything I wanted. Whatever job I applied for I got, whatever experience I wanted I could have, I was let out of more traffic tickets than I can count. Things are different on the outside. Job competition is fierce, there is a more balanced leadership and a notion that we all need to live peacefully together. There is a feeling of respect for one another if it is maintained mutually. We have neighbors of all different races, some working folks like ourselves, some not, some involved in questionable businesses out of their homes, others struggling to make ends meet with weekend yard sales. We nod to one another, but we do not get into each other's business. There is an unspoken sense of neighborhood, one of protection. If our neighbor needed help or they saw someone jump our fence, it would be taken care of. It is truly live and let live here, but we feel like we have got each other's back.

I am so grateful for my upbringing and will always love my hometown. Living away from it for a few years has allowed me to observe my own attitude and assumptions about others. It has helped me to understand different cultures and experience them as a majority, with my little white face poking in occasionally to learn more. I am not "there" yet, I still have a long way to go in my diversity education. But I no longer feel guilty. Now I feel like a support person. Someone who is here to take direction from those who know and help wherever they say the need is. Voting is my number one priority, speaking up is a close tie. Educating others about the true meaning of white privilege, and the changes that will need to be made to reverse the effects of colonialism are second on my list.

On the day I heard about the armed citizens in Yucaipa, threatening and intimidating protestors, I was not surprised, which made me feel sad. I want to believe that things will change. Yet, if parents are encouraging racism, then we are faced with another generation of it. I have seen so many reports of this, one example from 2019 as described in an article by Brian Whitehead. The article described an ongoing racial feud between Yucaipa High School and Rialto's Carter High School.

The players and coaches had just attended a sportsmanship symposium, which was to address the ongoing issues. "On Oct. 11, nine months after the sportsmanship symposium, a Yucaipa player shoved a Carter player while in the postgame handshake line and called him a racial slur, Paluba said. Later, Paluba added, a Yucaipa parent called a Carter player a derogatory word while on the field." (October 22, 2019, San Bernardino Sun).

This type of story is one of many about my hometown. It is not going to change until the school district, police department, city council and other leaders step up to recognize and acknowledge that there is a problem with racism in Yucaipa. It becomes difficult to envision such change, however, when the city's own mayor is stoking the fires of hatred.

In another San Bernardino Sun article written by Joe Nelson, revelations about Mayor Bobby Duncan's Facebook posts, his subsequent "apology," show the depth at which the racial attitude lies. One of the offensive posts from Duncan said, "I don't know about you, but I am 100% anti-Islam and anti-Sharia! Who else is with me and feels the same way?" Another of his posted memes shows the head of U.S. Rep. Ihan Omar, D-Minnesota, superimposed onto the body of a cobra, with a caption reading, "You knew what I was before you let me in." Another stated, "How do you walk 3,000 miles through Mexico 'without food or support' and wind up at the border 100 lbs. overweight and with cell phones?"

Most recently, on June 8th, the rumor of protestors heading toward Yucaipa sparked many business owners and citizens to line up along the street and on rooftops with guns to protect their town. Given the media portrayal of violence and destruction, looting, and conflict, it is understandable that there would be fear and a desire to protect themselves. The show of intimidation and absolute disrespect for the law is not acceptable, however. There are laws in the state against open carry. Yet, the restaurant brewery on Yucaipa Blvd, "Brewcaipa," had a crowd of citizens on the outdoor patio with guns in hand. A photo went viral on social media that appeared to show the ex-mayor with a gun alongside the citizens.

As reported by the Yucaipa News Mirror, "Yucaipa resident, Brenda Ebriham said,"... Yucaipa's leadership is actively gaslighting the city's residents regarding a photo that is currently being circulated on social media. This photo shows a council member, Bobby Duncan, sitting within arm's reach of an unattended firearm, propped in a chair, outside of Brewcaipa bar during a supposed city crisis. As we all know, California is not an open carry state. We also know there was never any credible threat to this city" Ebriham continued, "We are now being told that Bobby Duncan was not actually the owner of that firearm...It has been reported that YPD

(Yucaipa Police Department) asked that the gun be put away and Councilmember Duncan complied...Councilman Duncan should resign immediately. He has proven through his lack of decorum and abrasive vigilantism that he is unfit to represent the people of Yucaipa." (Michael Lopez and Rachel M. Gustuson, June 10, 2020).

Once again, a person in leadership has failed to set a good example of civilized and calm response to a situation that warrants a logical and delicate approach. If the leaders are not being responsible, then it condones irresponsible behavior in the citizenry. Here is the perfect opportunity for those who stand against racism and want to shed their white privilege to lead a strong campaign for this Council member's resignation. Freedom of thought and speech should always be protected, however when your position is a public one, supported by the taxpayers and by their will, whatever comes out of the public official's mouth should be neutral and non-inflammatory.

I am not so naive that I believe I can live in a place where racism does not exist and everything is unicorns and rainbows, but I will no longer keep silent when I see any behavior that prolongs the change most of us Americans long to see. It will be many generations before we fully eradicate bigotry and hatred of our fellow humans. My change in environment has helped me to grow, has opened my eyes to see the bigger picture. I have a long way to go, as I have stated many times. The generations of ingrained belief that "those poor people of color need our help" has perpetuated the stigma of helpless, ignorant humans who are less-than. No, instead they have been brought into a game of cards where the other side has a stacked deck and the pool is their lives.

We all must play the game in democracy, but for it to be truly an opportunity for everyone it must be fair in its rules and regulations. A bubble cannot last forever. It will eventually burst, and all sorts of stuff will spew forth. This is both good and bad. Good in the fact that we can see the ugly we need to clean up, bad in that the ugly fights for its life as it dies. Goodbye ugly, R.I.P.

What Can I Do?

The question "what can I do?" sounds loudly from those of us who want to do better but are not sure where to start. My husband Mike said, "I try to just treat everyone the same, I haven't done anything wrong, yet I feel a sense of blame. What more can I do?"

I recently read an article in *The Nation* online magazine written by Elie Mystal, and he suggested this:

"If you want to help me, be on my side. Not just during "protest week" but also during restaurant week and beach week and finals week and "I know a guy who has a yacht" week and all the weeks in between. Be one-tenth as pissed off about racism two weeks from now as I am every day, and let all your white friends know about it.

I do not need white validation of my rage. But I wouldn't object if more white people shared it. Go be angry at other white people for me, because some days I'd like to stay under the covers and hide from all your cops and crap."

(To the White People Who Keep Asking Me How to 'Help', Spare me the sympathy. It's the outrage that matters., June 3, 2020. https://www.thenation.com/article/society/white-people-anti-racism/)

There are many suggestions by people of color about how we can be of service. It seems, however, that the most important message is to stay involved, continue to change your own thoughts and speech, call your relatives or friends out when they make inappropriate remarks or spread ignorance and hate. Let them know that you are not okay with it. Silence is a form of agreement, as we all know. Keeping our mouth shut just to "not rock the boat" or upset a family member allows them to assume you agree with what they are saying. This is such a simple way of making a difference and being of service. It is kind of like smoking. When I was a kid every adult smoked. Throughout my life we have learned of the dangers of smoking, but it took society to see it as something undesirable in order to change anything. Smoking is now considered a dirty habit by many Americans, and fewer people do it. If we can make racism like smoking and eradicate it because it is not a healthy thing to live with, then we can progress as a society. It takes all of us to make it right.

As I have said, I'm still learning. I messed up a few months ago during a lunchtime discussion about hair at work. My male supervisor, who is black, was talking about our co-worker having such straight hair. She explained that she had to blow dry it and use products to get it that straight. I mentioned that my hair is naturally curly as well, and that I had to do the same thing. He argued, "But your hair moves, when I shake my head it doesn't move." There was added discussion about black women and their struggles with hairstyles that are "acceptable" in the workplace. It dawned on me later that my out of control curly long hair is never questioned no matter how I wear it. Plus, the texture is easily controlled using products and a blow dryer. I missed the entire point he was making. Black men and women are told to this day that their hair is "inappropriate" "extreme" or "too ethnic" according to their company's employee policies. My white privilege shows again, not only because of my ability to wear my hair anyway I want (other than, perhaps, non-natural color), but also in not "getting" the point of the conversation.

It's the little things, like bandages that come in all skin tones that can make such a difference. Imagine that one little change a company makes that can help children of color feel like they are noticed. How many white people ever considered what color bandages are? These are the types of things we can all advocate for. Inclusion is a small change that makes a huge difference. How hard is that to do? Consideration is not difficult.

Message to the Children

My great grandfather was born in Iowa in 1883. He lived with his parents on a farm in Iowa. Our country was in the midst of great expansion from east to west. Native peoples were being forced off their land and sent to live in new areas that were unfamiliar as reservations were built to keep them away from the civilized white settlers. At the same time, slavery had only been abolished twenty years earlier, and in many areas of the country Black families were trying to start over with nothing. Less than 150 years ago, five generations back, slavery was still legal and native people were being slaughtered. This was also a time when the Industrial Revolution was churning right along. Money and power began to run the country. One can look at this time in history as progress and assimilation, or as conquering and subjugation. Either is nothing to take pride in, however as a country with people united in determining a just and equal future, with strength and respect, we can find our patriotic pride once more.

There is a choice to be made. We can continue to operate in the old paradigm of racial hierarchy, or we can find our individual strength and combine it with that of our fellow humans to create a whole and perfect union that our forefathers would admire. My hope is that the next two generations will change the current narrative. It is imperative that they do. With pandemics, international unrest and climate change, there are profoundly important things that will need everyone's talent to control.

We can be a great nation once more, but it means changing everything. Rise up children, let us know how to help and let the world know that the United States is going through a metamorphosis of betterment. Send out your most smart, innovative, and level-headed peers to take on the task. The time for science and intellect to fully take the helm is now. Classrooms across the country should be teaching the truth about how this nation was conquered and built. Children need to learn non-sugarcoated version of colonialism, slavery, genocide, and manifest destiny. Protecting our white children from the truth about their forefathers does not help move our country forward. It only feeds the subconscious belief that they are superior.

Withholding science fact from children in certain areas of the nation due to religious beliefs is a "dumbing down" of knowledge and understanding about everything from mutation to natural selection to climate change. Children who are "sheltered" from secular intellect face a challenging world as adults. Some manage just fine and adapt well. Others may not react well at all. Young adults who are not equipped for independent critical thinking and problem solving have difficulty with integration and effective communication in the real world. This is best exemplified in a quote from the book Raising White Kids: Bringing Up Children in a Racial Unjust America by Jennifer Harvey (Abingdon Press, 2018).

She writes about a young child "singing the praises of George Washington when her mother explains that not all our country's historical leaders are innocent of doing wrong. The mother mentions the fact that Washington owned slaves and his fight for freedom was only for white people. The child responded, "But if he held slaves...why do we celebrate him as if he was such a great man?" The mother took the opportunity to ask her daughter how she felt about that.

The act of concealing historical fact in many areas of our country perpetuates the assumption of white supremacy. Part of learning how to help fight racism is to understand and accept this, then push for change in our nation's school curriculum. It is not enough for states to incorporate such a policy, it needs to be national. In fact, there should be certain courses about subjugation and indoctrination related to the spread of colonialism that are required for graduating high school.

These changes will not come easy, but they are not impossible. It will take white young adults working arm in arm with people of color to fertilize the racial understanding of the children of today. Marching, voting, speaking up are all great things to do, but until we acknowledge our privilege and ask how we may be of service to people of color, the root of racial injustice remains strong in the soil of America.

Yucaipa Valley, California
(photo credit: Cheryl Ann Hunter)

ABOUT THE AUTHOR

Cheryl Ann Hunter is a mother and grandmother, writer and artist living in southern California with her husband Mike.

A descendent of Scottish, English, and Irish immigrants, Cheryl is passionate about people, their origin, culture, belief system and personal stories that bring history to life. Her interest in social-cultural relationships and how societies develop their traditions inspire a desire to learn more about her fellow humans.

Discovering the truth about her own ancestors and the ways they stumbled through history, surviving to tell the story, helped Cheryl to understand the role they played in the darker parts of history.

Other books by this author, available at Amazon.com

Bottle or Breast? Only Mom Knows Best!

Paperback: 44 pages
Publisher: Independently published (June 9, 2020)
Language: English
ISBN-13: 979-8652384043
ASIN: B089TWSBFR
Product Dimensions: 6 x 0.1 x 9 inches

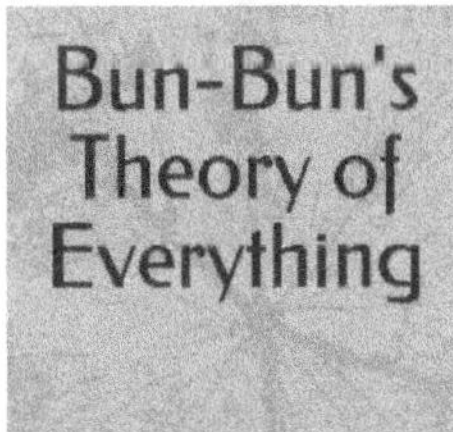

Bun-Bun's Theory of Everything

Paperback: 44 pages
Publisher: CreateSpace Independent Publishing Platform; 2 edition (July 11, 2014)
Language: English
ISBN-10: 1508578400
ISBN-13: 978-1508578406
Product Dimensions: 6.7 x 0.1 x 9.6 inches

Contact the author via email at:
Cheryl@CherylAnnHunter.com

Find her on Facebook and Instagram